CANADA

Whitecap
Vancouver / Toronto

Copyright © 1991 by Whitecap Books
Whitecap Books
Vancouver / Toronto

Text by Elaine Jones
Edited by Linda Ostrowalker
Cover and Interior design by Doug Smith

Typeset at CompuType, Vancouver, B.C.

Printed and bound in Canada by Friesen Printers, Altona, Manitoba

Canadian Cataloguing in Publication Data

Jones, Elaine.
  Canada

  ISBN 1-895099-51-X

  1. Canada—Description and travel—1981-
—Views. I. Title.
FC174.J65 1991   971.064′7′0222   C91-091260-2
F107.J65 1991

Frontispiece: The brilliant fall colours of a northern lake near Iron Bridge, Ontario.

Previous page: The old-world charm for which the city is famous is in evidence here in Mont Royal Park, Montreal.

Contents

Introduction

There is no simple way to characterize a land as vast as Canada. It is nearly 10 million square kilometres in area (over 3,800,000 square miles), the second largest country in the world. But it is not size alone that makes Canada remarkable. It is a land of extraordinary beauty, rich in natural resources, boasting a wide range of environments where abundant wildlife flourishes. Canada's people, too, are diverse. To its native people, Indian and Inuit, have been added a mixture of nationalities from every corner of the world, a cultural mosaic that adds richness and variety to the national character.

To the west lies the Pacific Ocean. Over 4,000 nautical miles of open ocean separate the western edge of the continent from the next point of land. Here wind and waves have helped sculpt a convoluted coastline of coves, bays, and steep-sided fiords. Offshore are a multitude of islands, ranging from Vancouver Island, the largest on the west coast of North America, to minute rocky islets inhabited only by cormorants and gulls. Warm ocean currents contribute to a year-round mild climate that is unique in Canada – a country where winter temperatures dip well below freezing in most areas. Heavy rainfall promotes the growth of lush coastal forests dominated by Douglas fir, cedar, and hemlock.

Inland, the continent folds in a series of mountain ranges that extend from the Pacific Ocean through British Columbia and into Alberta – the Coast Range, the Monashees, Selkirks, Columbia and Cariboo ranges, and, of course, the Rockies, straddling the border with Alberta. Some of Canada's most spectacular scenery is found here.

Beyond the mountains lie the great plains, stretching from the foothills of Alberta to the borders of Manitoba. By now the moisture-laden Pacific air has lost its water to the mountains. Weather on the prairies is typical of Canada's interior regions: cold in winter and hot and dry in the summer – sometimes too dry. But when spring and summer rains are sufficient, the fertile land, once a huge inland sea, produces bountiful crops ranging from wheat to canola, flax, sunflowers, and rye.

Opposite: Fall colours on a northern stretch of tundra, Yukon.

Above: Parliament Hill in Ottawa was opened in 1920, after a fire burned the original 1859 legislative buildings.

The lakes and vast forests of northern Ontario and Quebec give way in the south to Canada's most settled region. Concentrated around the Great Lakes and east along the Saint Lawrence River, this is Canada's most highly industrialized and populous area. Here, in central Canada, were fought the battles for sovereignty that eventually shaped Canada's future.

On the east, four of Canada's provinces – New Brunswick, Nova Scotia, Prince Edward Island, and Newfoundland – are bordered by the Atlantic Ocean. Bitterly cold and stormy in winter, the Atlantic has bred generations of strong, independent, seagoing people. The first known European exploration took place around the Grand Banks off Newfoundland, which drew Vikings as early as 1100 A.D. to fish the abundant cod.

To the north are vast, almost uninhabited tracts of land, from the boreal forests of the southern regions to Arctic tundra. Much of Canada's vast storehouse of natural resources is found in these northern reaches: pulp and paper from the forests, minerals from the earth, and hydroelectric power from its rivers. Characterized by twisting rivers, massive mountain ranges, and thousands of small lakes and islands, this vast wilderness is a paradise for outdoors enthusiasts. In its two northern territories, Yukon and Northwest Territories, the northern character of Canada is most profoundly felt.

Above: Sunlight hits the peak of Mount Edith Cavell, standing 3,363 metres high in Jasper National Park.

Opposite: Lighthouse at dawn, Stanhope, Prince Edward Island.

The West & the Yukon

The west is a broad term that encompasses foothills and mountains, ocean reaches and turbulent river systems, open plateaus and northern forests, villages, towns and thriving cities. At its farthest point, it is defined by the sea. Huge swells roll in from the Pacific, propelled by winds that blow over thousands of miles of unimpeded ocean. The inland waterways, deep fiords and the passages between outer islands and the mainland are safe anchorage for the fishing fleet and a paradise for recreational boaters.

Victoria, at the southernmost tip of Vancouver Island, enjoys some of the best weather in Canada and is known for its fabulous flowers, parks and gardens. Snowdrops and crocuses poke through the grass as early as February, and daffodils and cherry blossoms appear in March, marking the beginning of a season that lasts well into September.

Victoria, the provincial capital, is also known for its English atmosphere, enhanced by original turn-of-the-century architecture, tweed and linen shops, high tea at the Empress and horse-and-buggy tours.

Vancouver, across Georgia Strait, is British Columbia's largest city, with a population well over a million. A centre for business and development, its big-city atmosphere contrasts with the gentility of Victoria. Vancouver is also the gateway to an outdoors playground that includes varied water pursuits, world-class skiing, and a backyard wilderness that draws thousands of hikers, campers and outdoors enthusiasts each year.

Inland are the mountain ranges of the Western Cordillera and the flat upland plains of the Interior Plateau. Highways snake through the mountain passes, threads connecting the Pacific coast to the rest of the continent across the most formidable physical barrier in the country. Along the highways, settlements have sprung up around centres of farming, mining and forestry. In the hot, dry interior valleys, orchards and wineries prosper. Heavily

Opposite: Picturesque Emerald Lake is cradled in the mountains of Yoho National Park near the B.C.-Alberta border.

Above: The Empress Hotel overlooking Victoria Harbour reflects the essence of bygone Victorian elegance, from its architecture to its service.

forested slopes feed the province's number-one industry, forestry. In the interior valleys and plateaus, big spreads carry on a ranching tradition dating to the last century.

The Rocky Mountains, the easternmost of the ranges that make up the Cordillera, are not the tallest or the most rugged of Canada's mountains, yet they have exercised an almost mystical allure for travellers for hundreds of years. Two major national parks, Banff and Jasper, protect the wilderness and make it accessible to thousands of visitors annually. Connecting them is the Icefields Parkway, one of Canada's most stunning scenic drives, stretching for 230 kilometres (143 miles) from the Trans-Canada Highway near Lake Louise village north to Jasper townsite.

To the north is the Yukon, bordered to the west by Alaska. The gold rush of 1896 brought the Yukon to the world's attention and precipitated the first settlement. Today, its natural attractions – a wild, untamed beauty and a wide array of wildlife – are considered by many to be its most valuable treasure. The St. Elias Range contains the country's highest peak, 6,050-metre (19,850-foot) Mount Logan, and the most extensive glaciers outside the polar regions.

The population of the Yukon is just over 23,000, spread throughout about a dozen communities. The majority of its residents live in the capital city, Whitehorse, and enjoy an urban lifestyle and unparalleled natural surroundings. Dawson City, in its heyday the largest Canadian city west of Winnipeg, attracts many tourists each summer, who come to savour the lingering romance of the gold rush in the reconstructed town.

Above: The rural charm of Pitt Meadows, British Columbia, is enhanced by mountain views to the north.

Opposite: Island Lake in the Kootenays near Fernie, British Columbia, reflects surrounding mountain peaks and forested slopes.

Previous pages: The busy port of Tofino on Vancouver Island's western shore.

Above upper: Quathiaski Cove, Quadra Island, at daybreak.

Above lower: A misty sunrise at Long Beach, Pacific Rim National Park, on Vancouver Island.

Opposite: The Parliament Buildings dominate Victoria's inner harbour, particularly at night when they are brilliantly lit with thousands of lights.

Above: A ferry cuts through Active Pass en route to the mainland from Vancouver Island.

Opposite: Butchart Gardens is a renowned floral showplace near Victoria, British Columbia.

Opposite: The Lions Gate Bridge, spanning Burrard Inlet, is a well-known Vancouver landmark.

Above: Vancouver highrises catch the glow of a Pacific sunset.

Opposite: Spectacular Rocky Mountain vistas abound near Rogers Pass in Glacier National Park, British Columbia.

Above: Apple blossoms hold the promise of an abundant harvest in the Okanagan Valley near Penticton, British Columbia.

Previous page: Ranch country near Williams Lake, British Columbia.

Opposite: A windsurfer cuts across Okanagan Lake near Oyama, British Columbia.

Above upper: The rugged beauty of the Queen Charlotte Islands off British Columbia's coast.

Above lower: Sunset on the Kootenay River, British Columbia.

Above: The fertile fields of the Creston Valley, British Columbia.

Opposite: A working barn near Kamloops, British Columbia.

Opposite: Glaciers cap the dramatic Tombstone Mountains, Yukon.

Above: Aspen and spruce near the Alaska Highway at the Yukon-Alaska border.

Opposite: Rafting on the Firth River, Yukon.

Above: A camp tent near the Porcupine River, Yukon.

Opposite: Dawson City, Yukon was a thriving gold rush town at the turn of the century.

Above: The unparalleled beauty of a northern autumn sky, Yukon.

The Prairies and the Northwest Territories

Canada's great plains stretch across three provinces, from the foothills of Alberta, through Saskatchewan to the lake district of Manitoba, and encompass a surprising variety of environments. The northern parts of the prairie provinces are heavily forested, while the south ranges from rich agricultural lands to semiarid dunes, craggy badlands and dry grasslands.

Alberta is the land of the cowboy, although the modern version often uses a truck rather than the more traditional horse. A celebration of life on the range, the rodeo is still a major cultural event in the province, particularly the Calgary Stampede, which attracts top competitors and is known around the world. Calgary has always been a lively city that somewhat overshadowed the capital city, Edmonton. In the 1950s, the discovery of major oil deposits in the north gave Edmonton renewed life. With a population of 2,400,000, Alberta has more residents than the other two prairie provinces combined, and well over half of them live in these two cities. To the south are the badlands – deeply eroded mesas and canyons along riverbeds that are rich in fossils, particularly dinosaur bones. Dinosaur Provincial Park and Head-Smashed-In Buffalo Jump, near Fort Macleod, are designated international heritage sites.

Saskatchewan has long claimed the title "Bread Basket of the World," and is probably still best known for its wheat production. But the small farms have given way to large ones, agriculture has diversified, and the economy of the province is now augmented by petroleum, natural gas, potash and other mineral production. Regina is the capital of the province; its largest city is Saskatoon, located on the winding Saskatchewan River. Highways are now opening up the many lakes of the north to fishing and other wilderness pursuits. Cypress Hills Provincial Park is a surprising area of forest and grassland where species can be found that are unknown in the rest of the prairies.

Manitoba marks the boundary of the prairies and the beginning of the rugged forested rock formation called the Canadian Shield. While the southern part of the province shares the agricultural

Opposite: The Rocky Mountains loom in the distance over prairie farmlands at Pincher Creek, Alberta.

Above: The prairie harvest at sundown, Grandview, Manitoba.

31

soil of the prairies, more than half its area is a wilderness with a complex network of lakes and rivers, boreal forest, muskeg, and even Arctic tundra in its northernmost reaches. Hydroelectric power, forestry and extensive mineral resources are part of the riches of the province. An abundance of wildlife and thousands of lakes teeming with fish make Manitoba a popular destination for anglers and outdoors enthusiasts. Over half Manitoba's one million residents live in the capital city, Winnipeg. A rich cultural heritage from diverse nations finds free expression in Winnipeg, home of the Royal Winnipeg Ballet.

To the north lies the Northwest Territories, four times the size of the Yukon, but even more thinly populated. About 52,000 permanent residents live in more than sixty permanent communities, some consisting of only a few homes. Over half the population is made up of native Indian and Inuit people. The mining centre of Yellowknife, with over 20 percent of the population, has prospered since it became the capital in 1967.

Some of Canada's most rugged, powerful and glorious landscapes are found here. Nahanni National Park, in the southwest corner of the Northwest Territories, contains spectacular scenery, including Virginia Falls, more than twice the height of Niagara Falls. Located on Baffin Island's Cumberland Peninsula, Auyuittuq National Park is Canada's most northerly park and a true wilderness paradise.

Opposite: Spirit Island, sitting in the middle of Maligne Lake in Jasper National Park, imparts a mystical beauty.

Above: At Crowsnest Pass the highway cuts through the Rocky Mountains at the Alberta-British Columbia border.

Opposite: A row of grain elevators in Champion, Alberta, stands as testament to the prairie farmers' harvest.

Above: A flash of lightning illuminates the night sky above Edmonton, Alberta.

Above: An oil pump – a familiar sight throughout Alberta – works near Tilley in the southeast corner of the province.

Opposite: Sunlight gleams off the highrises of downtown Calgary, Alberta.

Previous page: Dinosaur Provincial Park, one of the world's most extensive dinosaur fossil fields, lies within Alberta's badlands along the Red Deer River.

Opposite: A sculpture entitled "Western Spirit" seemingly takes flight from downtown Regina, Saskatchewan.

Above: The Legislative Buildings in Regina, Saskatchewan, are reflected at night in the still waters of Wascana Lake.

Opposite: The Bessborough is one of Saskatoon's finest old hotels.

Above: A grain elevator in Weyburn, Saskatchewan, sends high-quality bread wheat on its way to international markets.

Opposite: A rock formation typical of Saskatchewan's badlands, seen at sunrise in Grasslands National Park.

Above: The clear brilliance of a northern summer day is captured at Prince Albert National Park, Saskatchewan.

Above: Echo Valley Provincial Park in the Qu'Appelle Valley, Saskatchewan.

Opposite: Undulating grain fields in southern Manitoba.

Opposite upper: The dome of Winnipeg's neoclassical Legislative Building features the famous Golden Boy statue, a symbol of the prairie spirit in Manitoba.

Opposite lower: Winnipeg is a visually and architecturally fascinating city, rich both in contemporary developments and in its well-preserved history.

Above: Grand Beach, on Lake Winnipeg's eastern shore, has one of the finest sand beaches in North America.

Above: The natural beauty of Reed Lake, near Flin Flon, Manitoba.

Opposite upper: Nueltin Lake is one of the myriad lakes in the Northwest Territories.

Opposite lower: Water plunges over Victoria Falls, on the Liard River in the Northwest Territories.

Opposite: Ice formations linger in July at the mouth of the Churchill River in northern Manitoba.

Above: Dog-sledding at Igloolik, Baffin Island.

Opposite: Mother and child, Foxe Basin, Baffin Island.

Above: Kayaks cut across a northern channel near Baffin Island.

Central Canada

Canada's largest provinces, Ontario and Quebec, are the heartland of industrial Canada. Manufacturing and the processing of natural resources are fuelled by the mineral-rich rock of the Canadian Shield – iron, uranium, copper, lead, zinc, nickel, cobalt, titanium, and asbestos. Much of Canada's population – 15,650,000 of its 25,309,000 residents – live in these two provinces.

Ontario, the second largest and most populous province, is a land of contrasts. Most of its population is clustered around the Great Lakes and on the narrow strip bordering the United States; about nine-tenths of the province is a virtually unpopulated wilderness of forests, lakes, and rivers. The southernmost point in Canada is located in Ontario: Point Pelee and its offshore islands, which extend into Lake Erie at the same latitude as northern California; fertile farmlands along the southern edge of the province produce peaches, wine grapes, and many other warm-weather crops. Nearly 1,600 kilometres (a thousand miles) north of here, polar bears roam a wilderness preserve at James and Hudson bays in the Arctic Ocean. There are large, busy, industrial cities, yet just a short distance away can be found quiet byways, with pastoral farmlands and small villages. Today its population pro-

vides yet another contrast. Not too long ago, Ontario was considered the preserve of the English in Canada. In the last few decades an influx of immigrants from every corner of the globe has added zest to the population mix.

Ontario has many large centres, but Toronto, the provincial capital, is the largest city at a metropolitan population of well over 3 million. The somewhat prim, decorous city of the last century has been replaced by a lively international centre that celebrates many cultures. The nation's capital, Ottawa, is a handsome city dominated by the grey stone construction and oxidized copper roofs of the Parliament Buildings. Situated across

Opposite: The countryside near Colborne, Ontario, on Lake Ontario is rich with rural heritage.

Above: Two of Toronto's best-known landmarks are the CN Tower – ''the world's tallest free-standing structure'' – and the SkyDome Stadium.

the Ottawa River from Hull in Quebec, these twin cities embody the bilingual nature of Canada, stemming from the two main streams of early European settlement, French and English.

From the sophistication of Montreal to historic Quebec City and the charming villages of the St. Lawrence lowlands, the French culture defines the province of Quebec.

Like Ontario, Quebec's population is centred around the south. Inroads have been made into the vast northern area for production of hydroelectric power, mining, and pulp and paper operations, but it remains almost uninhabited. The province's greatest

river, the St. Lawrence, is the vital link with the Atlantic. The complex engineering of the Great Lakes-St. Lawrence Seaway makes it possible to have a major seaport near Thunder Bay, over 3,200 kilometres (2,000 miles) from the Atlantic Ocean.

Montreal is Quebec's largest city, claiming almost 3 million of its 6,500,000 residents. It holds the unofficial title of Canada's most sophisticated city, conducting international business at fashionable venues and boasting a sparkling nighttime scene. The ancient walled town founded in 1608 is still to be found at the core of the capital, Quebec City. Narrow cobbled streets and tiny shops, horse-drawn buggy tours, and centuries-old architecture charm visitors to the capital, which is also a busy seaport and commercial centre.

Outside the major centres, the countryside of Quebec exhibits the rustic charm of centuries past. Pastoral hamlets are still dominated by church spires, the strip farms along the rivers date back to seigneurial times and the tiny fishing villages of the Gaspé Peninsula change little with the passage of time.

Above: Sunset at Blind River in northern Ontario.

Opposite: St. Andrews Church is one of the many charms of Niagara-on-the-Lake, Ontario.

Above: The town of Kenora is situated in the beautiful Lake of the Woods region in northern Ontario.

Opposite: The isolated beauty of the north shore of Lake Superior.

Previous page: Just outside of Ottawa in Richmond, Ontario, lie some of the province's richest farmlands.

Above: Army cadets carry out the traditional changing of the guard at Old Fort Henry, Kingston.

Opposite: Toronto's "new" City Hall (1965) and adjacent skating rink in Nathan Phillips Square contrast sharply with the Victorian Gothic stones of the Old City Hall of 1889.

Above: In Georgian Bay Islands National Park these distinctive rock formations are known as "flowerpots".

Opposite: The *Maid of the Mist* tour boat chugs through the churning waters below Niagara Falls.

Opposite: The Rideau Canal winds through the heart of Ottawa and falls to the Ottawa River below Parliament Hill.

Above: Stratford, Ontario is the home of one of North America's major theatre festivals, presenting world-class productions of works from Shakespeare to Gilbert and Sullivan.

Opposite: The spectacular La Chute waterfall in Forillon National Park, Gaspé Peninsula, Quebec.

Above: Grey, aging buildings contrast with the rich colours of fall in the countryside near Saint-Louis-du-Ha!-Ha!, Quebec.

Previous page: Bonaventure Island lies just offshore from Percé on the Gaspé Peninsula.

Opposite: A cathedral dominates the town of La Malbaie on the shores of the St. Lawrence in Quebec.

Above left: Notre Dame Church in Old Montreal, Quebec.

Above right: Old meets new throughout the sophisticated city of Montreal.

Previous pages: An ice-fishing colony at Sainte-Anne-de-la-Perade.

Opposite: Buildings dating from as early as the 17th century have been preserved in Old Quebec – the only walled city in America north of Mexico.

Above: A cool lake reflects warm autumn colours in the Laurentians, Quebec.

Opposite: Eel weirs on the St. Lawrence River at Kamouraska, Quebec.

Above: A well-known landmark, Percé Rock is a 288-foot-high (86 m) naturally formed citadel of limestone, with a 60-foot (18 m) wave-carved arch within.

Atlantic Canada

Almost half of Canada's provinces – four out of ten – are on the Atlantic. They vary from the tiniest, Prince Edward Island, 5,656 square kilometres (2,184 square miles) in size and tucked into the continent, to Newfoundland, the last province to join Confederation, in 1949, and one which remains somewhat isolated by distance and custom from the mainland. All share one overwhelming factor: the powerful, dangerous, and bountiful Atlantic Ocean.

New Brunswick, one of the four original provinces in the Canadian Confederation, is rich in history. Many of the early settlers were United Empire Loyalists who fled the newly independent United States, and the connection with the United States is still strong today. Bordered on the west by Quebec, there is also a strong French influence and the province is officially bilingual. Much of the population of the province settled along the Saint John River, one of the most beautiful waterways in Canada. The capital, Fredericton, and largest city, Saint John, are both located on the river, which empties into the Bay of Fundy. The majority of the province is heavily forested, providing one of the mainstays of the economy; picturesque fishing and farming communities dot the coastline.

Nova Scotia is connected to mainland New Brunswick only by a narrow isthmus. It is truly a maritime province: no part of it is far from the sea and the deeply indented coastline provides a multitude of harbours for the fishing fleet – including one of the most famous, Peggy's Cove. Cape Breton Island is separated from the rest of Nova Scotia by the narrow Strait of Canso, and is itself divided by an inland sea, Bras d'Or Lake. This convoluted coastline gives Nova Scotia a claim to having some of the world's finest scenic and recreational areas. Canada's first permanent settlement was here at Port Royal, today commemorated in a national historic park. Halifax, capital of the province, is a busy port city that successfully combines old and new.

Opposite: A row of heritage buildings are highlighted by the sun in Pictou, Nova Scotia.

Above: The unmistakable colour and flavour of the Maritimes are captured here in Blue Rocks, Nova Scotia.

The fertile red soil and green fields of Prince Edward Island have given it the well-deserved title of "Canada's Garden Province" – or "Spud Island" to the less reverent. The most densely populated of all the provinces, almost all of its land is arable – as well as the traditional potato farms, the island produces a variety of other crops. Fishing is its secondary industry; the island is especially famed for its lobsters and Malpeque oysters. Tourism also plays a part in the economy; visitors are attracted to the quiet country atmosphere and red sand beaches. Charlottetown is the capital and largest city. One of the older Canadian cities, it retains much of the charm of earlier eras.

Newfoundland and Labrador is comprised of the island of Newfoundland, at the mouth of the Gulf of St. Lawrence, and its mainland territory of Labrador. Labrador is relatively unsettled but is important for its mineral and forest resources. The rocky shores of Newfoundland have a severe beauty that seems to capture the hearts of those who live or visit there. Fishing has always been the main resource; since the time of the Vikings, sailors have been braving the Atlantic for the cod that school off the Grand Banks. The tiny fishing villages, or outports, that developed remained virtually unchanged over the centuries, preserving British dialects that disappeared in their original homeland. Even today, many Newfoundlanders retain their unique culture. The capital city, St. John's, is the major harbour for the Newfoundland fleet.

Opposite: Spring blossoms adorn the grounds of Evangeline Park Church, Grand Pré, Nova Scotia.

Above: The city's skyline is mirrored in the waters of Halifax harbour, a busy international seaport.

Opposite: Picturesque Peggy's Cove is the quintessential Nova Scotian fishing village.

Above: Originally built by the French in 1744, the fortress of Louisbourg on Cape Breton Island has been reconstructed and furnished to the period.

Previous page: A stretch of rugged coastline at Red Point Beach, Prince Edward Island.

Opposite: Fishing buoys lean against a stack of lobster traps on Cape Breton Island, Nova Scotia.

Above: North Lake, Prince Edward Island, is a major port for deep-sea fishermen seeking the giant bluefin tuna.

Opposite: The gentle beauty of Prince Edward Island's farmlands, near New Glasgow.

Above upper: In Cavendish, Prince Edward Island, sits the farm made famous as the setting for Lucy Maud Montgomery's well-loved novel, *Anne of Green Gables*.

Above lower: Province House in Charlottetown, Prince Edward Island, was the site of Canada's Confederation conference in 1864. It is still used as the province's legislature.

Opposite: The sawmill at Kings Landing near Fredericton, New Brunswick, is part of a heritage site depicting an early Loyalist settlement.

Above: Campobello Island, New Brunswick, is famous as the summer home of Franklin D. Roosevelt.

Above: The old English character of St. Andrews, New Brunswick, is reflected in the half-timbered grandeur of the Algonquin Hotel.

Opposite: ''Flowerpot'' rock formations have been carved by the action of the Bay of Fundy tides near Hopewell, New Brunswick.

Opposite: Colourful skiffs lined up on the shore at Northern Head on Grand Manan Island, New Brunswick.

Above upper: The lighthouse at Lobster Cove, Newfoundland.

Above lower: The dramatic fiords at Gros Morne National Park show Newfoundland's natural beauty at its best.

Above: Elegant brownstones on a street in Saint John, New Brunswick – Canada's oldest incorporated city.

Opposite: The detail and colour treatment of this gabled window give it a distinctly Maritime flavour.

Above upper: Sunrise at Gros Morne National Park on Newfoundland's west coast.

Above lower: One of the oldest cities in North America, St. John's, Newfoundland, is distinguished by unique and colourful architecture.

Opposite: Like so many of Newfoundland's seaports, Port-aux-Basques clings to rocky ground.

Above: Sunset is reflected on the snow-covered mountains in northern Labrador.

Opposite: A young Inuit boy in Nain, Labrador.

Above: Nain, Labrador, is dwarfed by its icy surroundings.